D0099649

This item is a gift
from the

Friends of the Danville Library

DRAWING MANGA

WEAPONS, VEHICLES, AND ACCESSORIES

ANNA SOUTHGATE
AND KEITH SPARROW

rosen publishing's
rosen
central
NEW YORK

WITHDRAWN

This edition published in 2012 by:

The Rosen Publishing Group, Inc.
29 East 21st Street
New York, NY 10010

Additional end matter copyright © 2012 by The Rosen Publishing Group, Inc.

All rights reserved. No part of this book may be reproduced in any form without permission in writing from the publisher, except by a reviewer.

Library of Congress Cataloging-in-Publication Data

Southgate, Anna.
Drawing manga weapons, vehicles, and accessories / Anna Southgate, Keith Sparrow.—1st ed.
    p. cm.—(Manga magic)
Includes bibliographical references and index.
ISBN 978-1-4488-4801-0 (library binding)
ISBN 978-1-4488-4805-8 (pbk.)
ISBN 978-1-4488-4809-6 (6-pack)
1. Comic books, strips, etc.—Japan—Technique—Juvenile literature. 2. Cartooning—Technique—Juvenile literature. I. Sparrow, Keith. II. Title. III. Series.
NC1764.5.J3S68 2011
741.5'1—dc22

2011010682

Manufactured in the United States of America

CPSIA Compliance Information: Batch #S11YA: For further information, contact Rosen Publishing, New York, New York, at 1-800-237-9932.

All other content copyright © 2007 Axis Publishing Limited, London.

CONTENTS

INTRODUCTION

You've drawn the perfect manga magical princess. She has bright blue eyes and bright blue hair to match and a royal stance. You've even tailored the perfect dress, leggings, and boots for a dimension-traveling princess. But something's still missing: the accessories! Give your princess a magic scepter and tiara adorned with a glowing crystal, and you've now taken a good manga character and transformed her into a great character, unique and detailed.

Drawing cool accessories for your manga creations gives your creations more depth and sets them apart from other characters. These accessories can be gadgets and gear, eye patches, scarves, or even tails. Knowing how to draw tools and weapons may also be essential to your storytelling. After all, what kind of ninja doesn't have throwing stars? Helmets and headgear, bracelets, earrings, and other jewelry, gloves and gauntlets, and glasses and goggles are just some of the objects to inspire you as you learn to draw.

With manga vehicles, the sky's the limit. If you can imagine it, you can draw it, because the technical details aren't as important when you are drawing. In real life, your airship might never get off the ground, but follow these tips and it'll look like it's ready to take on an armada of space pirates, no problem! The step-by-step instructions in this book will show you the way to crafting weaponry, accessories, and vehicles.

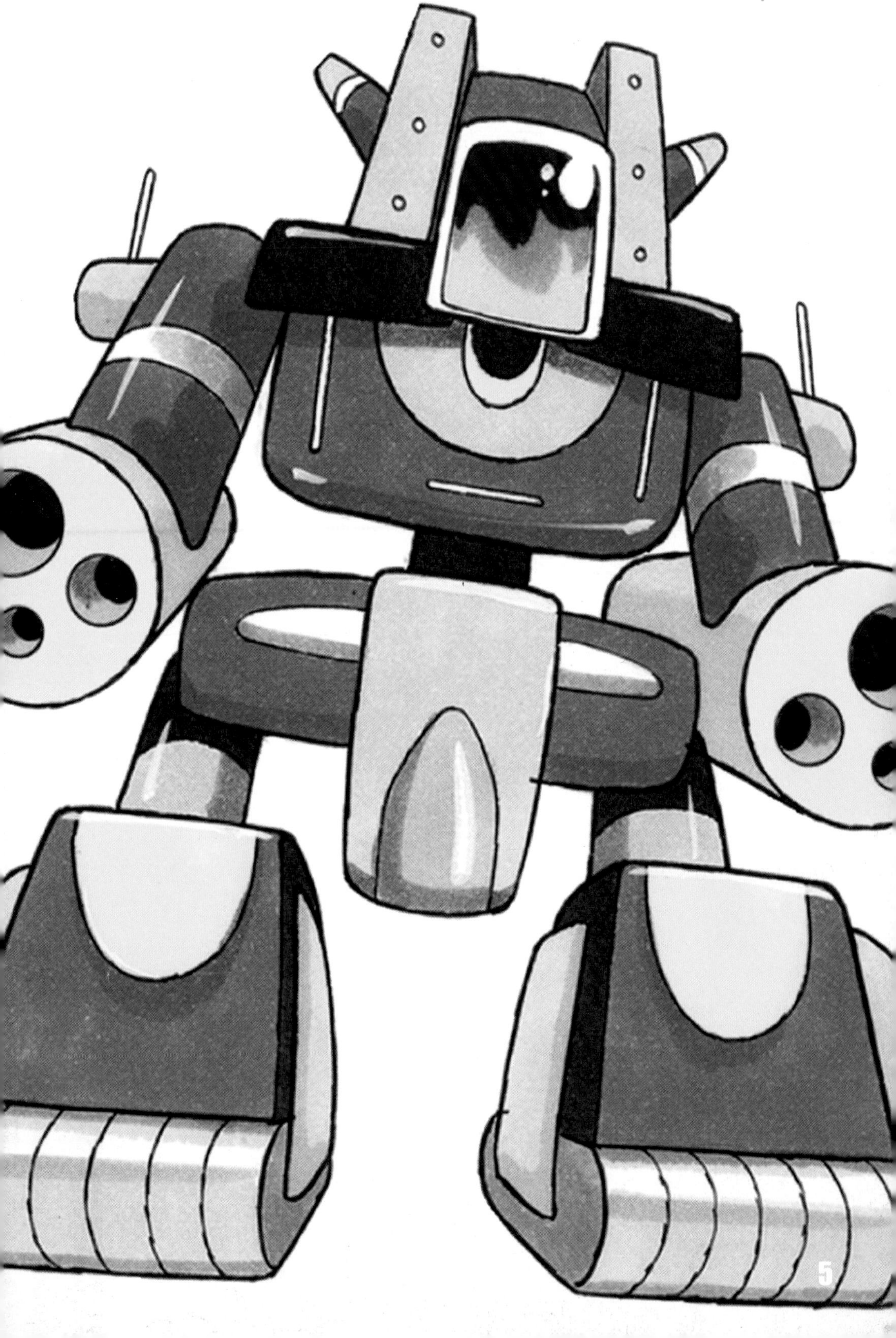

You do not need to spend a fortune to get started drawing and coloring good manga art. You do, however, need to choose your materials with some care to get the best results from your work. Start with a few basics and add to your kit as your style develops and you figure out what you like working with.

Artists have their preferences when it comes to equipment, but regardless of personal favorites, you will need a basic set of materials that will enable you to sketch, ink, and color your manga art. The items discussed here are only a guide—don't be afraid to experiment to find out what works best for you.

PAPER

You will need two types of paper—one for creating sketches, the other for producing finished color artwork.

For quickly jotting down ideas, almost any piece of scrap paper will do. For more developed sketching, though, use tracing paper. Tracing paper provides a smooth surface, helping you to sketch freely. It is also forgiving—any mistakes can easily be erased several times over. Typically, tracing paper comes in pads. Choose a pad that is around 24 pounds (90 grams per square meter) in weight for best results—lighter tracing paper may buckle and heavier paper is not suitable for sketching.

Once you have finished sketching out ideas, you will need to transfer them to the paper you want to produce your finished colored art on. To do this, you will have to trace over your pencil sketch, so the paper you choose cannot be too opaque or heavy—otherwise you will not be able to see the sketch underneath. Choose a paper around 16 lb (60 gsm) for this.

Graphite pencils are ideal for getting your ideas down on paper and producing your initial drawing. The pencil drawing is probably the most important stage in creating your artwork. Choose an HB and a 2B to start with.

The type of paper you use is also important. If you are going to color using marker pens, use marker or layout paper. Both of these types are very good at holding the ink found in markers. Other paper of the same weight can cause the marker ink to bleed, that is, the ink soaks beyond the inked lines of your drawing and produces fuzzy edges. This does not look good.

You may wish to color your art using other materials, such as colored pencils or watercolors. Drawing paper is good for graphite pencil and inked-only art (such as

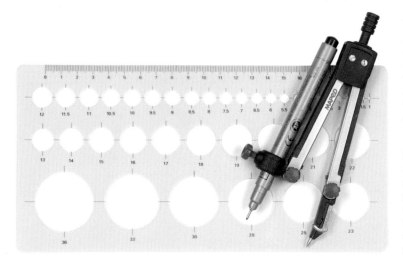

Working freehand allows great freedom of expression and is ideal when you are working out a sketch, but you will find times when precision is necessary.

Use compasses or a circle guide for circles and ellipses to keep your work sharp. Choose compasses that can be adjusted to hold both pencils and pens.

that found in the majority of manga comic books), while heavyweight watercolor paper holds wet paint and colored inks and comes in a variety of surface textures.

Again, don't be afraid to experiment: you can buy many types of paper in single sheets until you find the ones that suit your artwork best.

PENCILS

The next step is to choose some pencils for your sketches. Pencil sketching is probably the most important stage, and always comes first when producing manga art (you cannot skip ahead to the inking stage), so make sure you choose pencils that feel good in your hand and allow you to express your ideas freely.

Pencils are manufactured in a range of hard and soft leads. Hard leads are designated by the letter H and soft leads by the letter B. Both come in six levels—6H is the hardest lead and 6B is the softest. In the middle is HB, a halfway mark between the two ranges. Generally, an HB and a 2B lead will serve most sketching purposes, with the softer lead being especially useful for loose, "idea" sketches, and the harder lead for more final lines.

Alternatively, you can opt for mechanical pencils. Also called self-propelling pencils, these come in a variety of lead grades and widths, and never lose their points, making sharpening traditional wood-cased pencils a thing of the past. Whether you use one is entirely up to you—it is possible to get excellent results whichever model you choose.

SHARPENERS AND ERASERS

If you use wooden pencils, you will need to get a quality sharpener; this is a small but essential piece of equipment. Electric sharpeners work very well and are also

Felt-tip pens are the ideal way to ink your sketches. A fineliner, medium-tip pen and sign pen should meet all of your needs, whatever your style and preferred subjects. A few colored felt-tip pens can be a good addition to your kit, allowing you to introduce color at the inking stage.

very fast; they last a long time, too. Otherwise, a handheld sharpener is fine. One that comes with a couple of spare blades can be a worthwhile investment, to ensure that your pencils are always sharp.

Along with a sharpener, you will need an eraser for removing any visible pencil lines from your inked sketches prior to coloring. Choose a high-quality eraser that does not smudge the pencil lead, scuff the paper, or leave dirty fragments all over your work. A soft putty eraser works best, since it absorbs pencil lead rather than just rubbing it away. For this reason, putty erasers do become dirty with use. Keep yours clean by trimming it carefully with scissors every now and then.

INKING PENS

The range of inking pens can be bewildering, but some basic rules will help you select the pens you need. Inked lines in most types of manga tend to be quite bold, so buy a thin-nibbed pen, about 0.5 mm (.02 inches) and a medium-size nib, about 0.8 mm (.03 inches). Make sure that the ink in the

pens is waterproof; this ink won't smudge or run. Next, you will need a medium-tip felt pen. Although you won't need to use this pen very often to ink the outlines of your characters, it is still useful for filling in small detailed areas of solid black. The Pentel sign pen does this job well. Last, consider a pen that can create different line widths according to the amount of pressure you put on the tip. These pens replicate brushes and allow you to create flowing lines such as those seen on hair and clothing. The Pentel brush pen does this very well, delivering a steady supply of ink to the tip from a replaceable cartridge.

Test-drive a few pens at your art store to see which ones suit you best. All pens should produce clean, sharp lines with a deep black pigment.

MARKERS AND COLORING AIDS

Many artists use markers, rather than paint, to color their artwork, because markers are easy to use and come in a huge variety of colors and shades. Good-quality markers, such as those made by Chartpak, Letraset, or Copic, produce excellent, vibrant results, allowing you to build up multiple layers of color so you can create rich, detailed work and precise areas of shading. Make sure

Markers come in a wide variety of colors, which allows you to achieve subtle variations in tone. In addition to a thick nib for broad areas of color, the Copic markers shown here feature a thin nib for fine detail.

that you use your markers with marker or layout paper to avoid bleeding. Markers are often refillable, so they last a long time. The downside is that they are expensive, so choose a limited number of colors to start with, and add as your needs evolve. As always, test out a few markers in your art store before buying any.

However, markers are not the only coloring media. Paints and gouache also produce excellent results, and can give your work a distinctive look. Add white gouache, which comes in a tube, to your work to create highlights and sparkles of light. Apply it in small quantities with a good-quality watercolor brush.

It is also possible to color your artwork on a computer. This is quick to do, although obviously there is a high initial cost. It also tends to produce flatter color than markers or paints.

DRAWING AIDS

Most of your sketching will be done freehand, but there are situations, especially with man-made objects such as the edges of buildings or the wheels of a car, when your line work needs to be crisp and sharp to create the right look. Rulers, circle guides, and compasses all provide this accuracy. Rulers are either metal or plastic; in most cases, plastic ones work best, though metal ones tend to last longer. For circles, use a circle guide, which is a plastic sheet with a wide variety of different-sized holes stamped out of it. If the circle you want to draw is too big for the circle guide, use a compass that can hold a pencil and inking pen.

A selection of warm and cool grays is a useful addition to your marker colors and most ranges feature several different shades. These are ideal for shading on faces, hair, and clothes.

ACCESSORIES

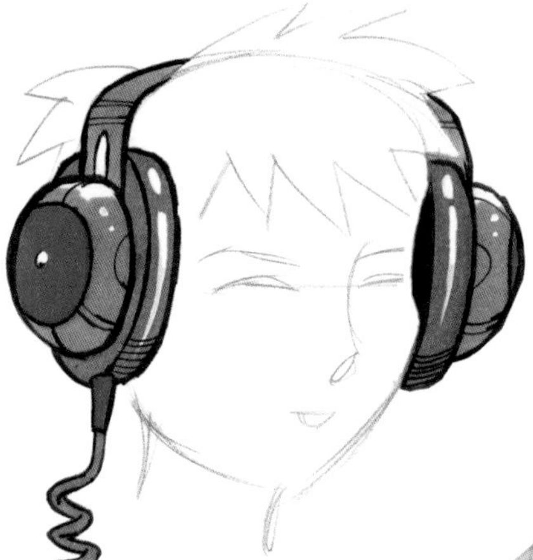

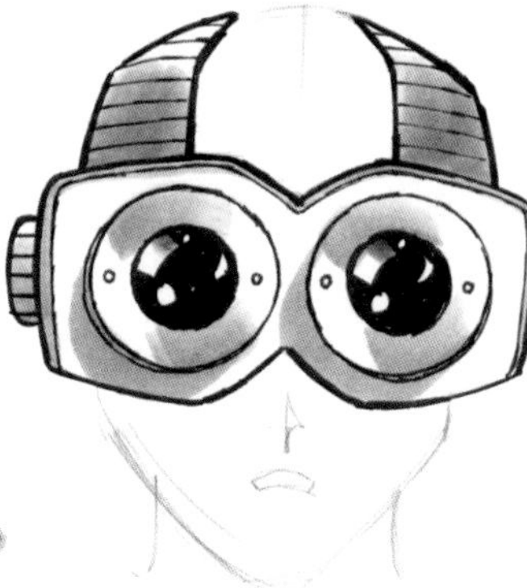

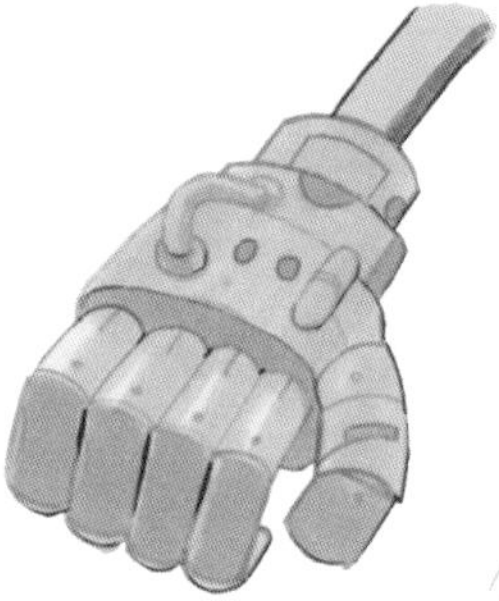

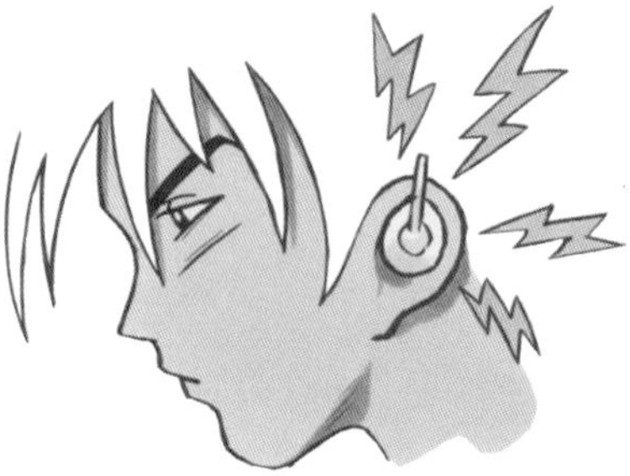

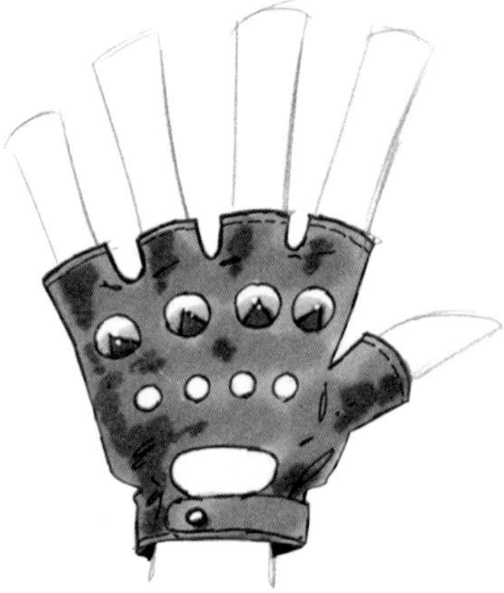

You can have a lot of fun with accessories and gadgets, and it is worth practicing drawing them. A simple touch such as a helmet or belt can really make a character stand out, and give him or her (or it!) a unique identity. Use the examples here as starting points: there is no limit to your imagination in devising accessories.

BASEBALL CAP

The baseball cap is one of the most common forms of headgear, and is easy to draw. Hats can be a useful accessory to individualize a character. This one is a standard shape, with a curving peak and a vent at the back. The panels of the cap alternate between yellow and white, and there is a white button on top.

Start with a basic head shape, and establish an eye line.

Sketch in positions for the eyes, nose, and mouth, then draw a line circling the head just above the eyeline.

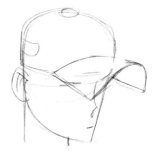

Then establish the lines of the cap's peak: these consist of two curves and two horizontals. Add in the vent detail, and the button on the crown.

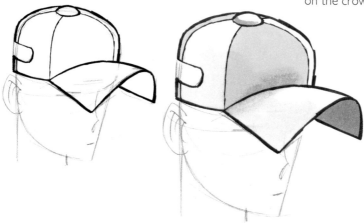

Ink the lines you established in pencil using a medium nib, then with a thinner nib outline stitching lines on the crown.

Establish two areas of yellow, leaving two white. Create a gray shadow on the button, with a deeper gray under the peak.

HEADPHONES

Headgear isn't just about hats. This character wears large, old-fashioned head-phones with cushioned earpieces. He could be a music-loving teen, a helicopter pilot, or somebody on surveillance duty at a stake-out.

Create a basic oval head, adding a curving line on the right to get the eyeline on that side of the face. This helps you to get the lines of the pad later.

Add basic features of eyes and brows, nose, and mouth. Then create the ovals of the pads on both sides of the head.

The phones and pads are constructed from circles and ovals in perspective. Add the lines of the headpiece, and a curly electrical cord. Finally sketch in some hair.

Ink the main lines you have established, varying the thickness of the nib for the different areas of the headphones and pads.

Leaving white highlights, color the pads gray. Use brown for the headpiece, headphones, and electrical cord, with red for the detailing.

TECH SPECS

Eyewear is another good accessory for your manga characters. These are serious-looking glasses with a tinted visor, and a heavy, metallic frame that looks like it could contain some electronic hardware. Note how the tint on the lens is a gradient, which gives it extra realism.

Draw a basic head shape using a circle and curving lines down to the chin, and indicate two vertical lines for the neck.

Sketch in the eyes, ears, nose and mouth, then draw a curving horizontal band across the top of the eye level.

From here, add the lines of the lenses, which are essentially half circles. Create the large joints for the earpieces, then give the character some spiky hair.

Ink the lines of the eyes, and then all the main lines of the frame, earpieces, and lenses.

Leaving white highlights to suggest reflections, color the lenses brown. Then use a mauve gray for details on the crosspieces and earpiece, with ice blue above the nose.

SPY GOGGLES

Goggles are another form of eyewear. They could be night-vision or infrared. The straps sit across the top of the head to give a firm fit, and the dials on either side of the goggles may be used for focus or mode switching. The lenses are large, camera-like pieces for a powerful look.

Start with a circular shape for the head, then draw two curving lines down to a pointed chin. Add two short verticals for the neck.

Draw a horizontal for the eye and ear line, with a vertical center line. Position the nose and mouth, then draw two circles for the goggles' lenses.

Add more detail of the frames with two larger circles, then create the shape of the frame. Add earpieces, then work some details into the head.

Ink all the lines, using two thick-nesses of nib. Then use black ink to color the lenses, leaving three white highlights in each.

Introduce color into the headpieces and around the lenses, frame, and earpieces. Then use gray for shadow areas around the lenses and under the eyepieces.

HEADBAND

This scarlet sash tied around the head can give your character a touch of drama and bravery. It can be a good accessory for a warrior or street fighter, or just someone with a devil-may-care attitude to life. Note how the shading with horizontal lines gives the fabric a realistic look.

Draw a circle for the head, with two curving lines down to a pointed chin. Add a horizontal for the neck.

Now add horizontals to help position the eyes and eyebrows, and two more for the top and bottom of the headband. Add a nose and a mouth.

Create the ear, using the eyeline as a guide to position. Then give the character thick spikes of hair on top of the head. Finally, create the rounded lines of the headband.

Ink the folds and creases of the headband, creating some thick lines to give it some texture.

Finally, color the headband bright red.

NINJA-STYLE HEADWRAP

A more austere look is this all-over head-and-neck wrap, in the style of a ninja warrior. Ninjas usually favor dark colors such as black, dark blue, and dark red, but can also wear white and other colors. Usually the lower half of the face is also covered, but here the look is open-faced. Note the white highlights across the forehead, which give a full, rounded look.

Start with a circle, then draw two lines down to a pointed chin. Create the profile of the chin, then add lines for the neck.

Add a horizontal eyeline, then position eyes, eyebrows, nose, and mouth. Refine the jawline, then add the horizontal for the bottom of the headpiece.

Create the profile of the headpiece by sharpening the line of the crown, and creating two verticals for the sidepiece. Then add its line under the chin.

Use a medium-nibbed pen to ink the main lines of the profile of the headpiece, and then add some ink lines to suggest folds and creases in the fabric.

Leave some areas of white highlight on top of the head to help with modeling, then color the headpiece dark blue. Add darker color down the sides and under the chin.

17

FINGERLESS FIGHTING GLOVES

These studded leather gloves are good for a tough, streetwise character who may be a gang member or otherwise involved in violent activities. The knuckles are studded with short metallic spikes and the fingers are left open for extra flexibility.

Draw a hand from basic shapes, with four simple rounded rectangles for fingers.

Create the shape of the fingerless glove. Draw the line of the cuff with a stud detail. Add circles for the knuckles and for the glove details.

Ink over all the lines to outline the shape of the glove. Ink the knuckle detail, then suggest some creasing around the wristline and the bottom of the fingers.

Color the glove purple-gray, then add darker grays for shadows and texture. Use a pale blue to add a hint of steel to the studs on the knuckle line.

EXOTIC RINGS

This colorful collection of rings could be ideal for a fantasy story with a wizard or sorcerer of some kind. Each ring looks magical in its own way, and the ring on the little finger has a skull-like motif to convey an air of danger. The brightly colored centerpieces on the other rings have multiple white highlights to show reflections.

Draw a basic fist using right angles for the fingers. Add the joints of the closest finger, and outline the thumb.

Add a fantasy ring to each finger, diminishing in size from the first finger down to the little finger.

Ink the major lines of the rings, outlining all the details you worked up in pencil.

Color your rings using a variety of colors. Leave white highlights. Finally, work up some gray shadows to suggest that the rings are metallic.

GALLERY

bracelet

below This bracelet has a decorative, traditional look, but it could also be turned into a futuristic weapon.

cute pet

above If all else fails, nothing works better than a sidekick. A colorful pet such as this provides a confidant for the character, and offers plenty of opportunities for laughs.

gauntlet

below This looks like a weapon. The dull gray color gives a no-nonsense, functional look.

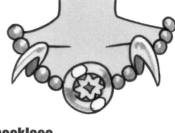

necklace

above This necklace could grace a tribal queen in official dress. The gold gives an air of wealth, but the curved spikes look like teeth from a jungle beast.

winged hat

below The owner of this baseball cap with its quirky twist could be a fun-loving teen.

belt

above This belt has a colorful, military-style buckle, and could be part of a uniform.

strap

right A big leather strap and buckle is great for a swash-buckler or a pirate.

goggles

above These look like they are serious night-vision hardware. Goggles can add a great deal to any street character.

earrings

right Earrings such as this one have a rebellious, nonconformist feel, especially when they are added to a pointy ear.

WRISTBAND

Here is a weighty-looking wristband or bracelet. The extra-thick shape has a series of what appear to be carved grooves, which give a suggestion of technology, but the texture and color look almost stonelike and primitive. It could be an alien artifact, or a relic discovered on an archaeological dig. The fist implies it is a weapon of some kind, though.

Start with a basic fist, created from angled lines. Add a sausage-shaped thumb across the fingers.

Now create the outline of a chunky wristband from circular lines. Make one tight around the wrist, and two more to give it a profile. Add chevron patterns and some circle details.

Ink the wristband, including the details. Then ink around the wrist to establish the inner profile of the wristband.

Color the wristband yellow, then work up the details in a more golden shade. Create brown shadows under the wristband.

CLAWS

Give your manga character a feral, animal look with these dangerous-looking claws. They extend in long curves out from each fingernail, and are colored shiny black for extra menace. The fingers here are slender and feminine, which suggests a catlike attitude.

Start with a basic open hand with four fingers and a thumb.

Now draw superlong pointed fingernails from all the fingers and the thumb, starting from the rounded cuticles.

Outline the areas of fingernail using black ink.

Leaving areas of white highlight on each nail, color them shiny black.

POWER GAUNTLET

This is a heavyweight piece of hardware, with a hefty metallic gauntlet studded with what could be lasers or projectile launchers. The fingertips are open to enable a more delicate control, and the back of the hand appears to have a main firing button.

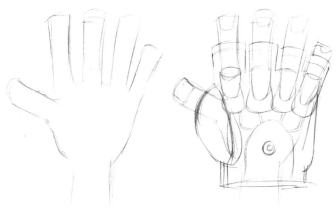

Draw a hand using basic shapes. making the back, wrist, fingers, and thumb.

Now create the outline of the gauntlet. Take the fingers up to the first joints, work some detailing around the base of the fingers, and add a shield shape to the back of the hand.

Ink over all the detailed lines you worked in pencil, including the fine lines at the ends of the fingers of the glove. Then ink the shields on the joints and back of the hand, and the jewel.

Keep the color minimal. Color the jewel setting ice blue, and use blue for the line details and finger studs. Then use mauve to get some rounded modeling into the hand and fingers, and onto the thumb. Finally add gray shading around the wrist.

GOLDEN BANGLE

This finely crafted bangle is made from pure gold, and would be a fitting decoration for a manga princess or royalty of some kind, as suggested by the slender, feminine hand and wrist. The shape is simple and elegant, with a cut-away ellipse on the back, and large gold studs circling the wrist.

Create a basic hand with a long, slender wrist, back of the hand, and four fingers.

Now draw a fine, broad bracelet around the wrist. Give it a U-shaped detail, then add two full studs and the profiles of two more for its decoration.

Ink the outline of the bracelet, its U-detail profile, and studs. Then ink darker areas on both sides to suggest modeling. Create shadow around the wrist.

Use honey gold to strengthen the effect of a metal bracelet. Leave areas white on the bracelet and the studs, to suggest their rounded shapes.

DEMON TAIL

An appendage like this demonic-looking tail can be a great way to give your character a memorable and unusual accessory. It has a slightly devilish look, but does not necessarily imply an evil personality and can just as readily be used on a cute, monkeylike figure.

Create a body from basic shapes, fleshing out the arms and legs so that you have the running profile of a figure.

Draw a curling S-shape up and out from the buttocks. Flesh this out with a line on either side, then give it a pointed end.

Start inking from above the buttocks, taking the line up the tail, around the point, and back into the buttock. Start a new line to create the top of the leg.

Use two shades of reptilian green, with some white modeling to make the shape of the tail.

TRIBAL AMULET

If your character is in a primitive tribal setting, or perhaps in a rural historical scenario, she may be wearing something like this amulet. There are a pair of chunky-looking gemstones, fixed by leather straps into a neck ornament.

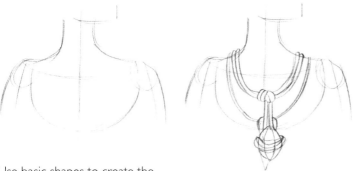

Use basic shapes to create the outline of shoulders, neck, and upper chest. Flesh out the upper arms, and add a breastline.

Start with a string of three curving lines, then add two deeper curved lines. Hang a thin triangle from the bottom string, add an oval detail, then create a knotted detail to join the two.

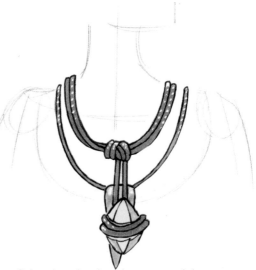

Ink the lines in the order you drew them: the knot on the upper string should read in front of the triangle, and the strings on the lower sit beneath it.

Color the triangle pale green and the upper jewel in shades of gold. Then make all the strings leather-colored. Finally, add some tiny white highlights to the leather thongs.

CAT EARS

A peculiar feature of manga stories is the way some characters sport random animal characteristics, such as these catlike ears. Sometimes these features are used to denote a certain quirky personality trait, and sometimes to signify an alien race or fantasy humanoid. The ears can be worn in tandem with a tail for extra effect, but the figure would be otherwise human.

Draw an oval, then refine its profile. Add a horizontal for the eyeline, then draw large, innocent eyes. Add a tiny nose and mouth.

Starting from the line at the top of the head, outline two triangular ears, with inner ears. Then create a short, spiky fringe, and body of hair.

Ink the two sets of lines for both ears, and then ink the line at the base on the ear on the right.

Color the outer ears brown and the inner ear pale pink.

FANTASY HELMET

Here's another character with animalistic ears, this time with the added accessory of a fantastical-looking helmet. The ears resemble a kid goat, and the hat is reminiscent of a toadstool, so the overall effect is cute and whimsical, and would suit a fantasy tale of woodland folk perhaps.

Start with an oval for the head. Add a curved horizontal and position large eyes with highlights on it. Add a tiny nose, mouth, and ear.

Work a double line out from the center of the head on both sides to create the brim. Add a domed profile, with central trim. Add button details down this trim.

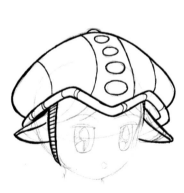

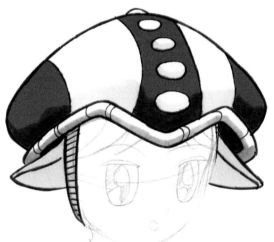

Ink all the main lines of the profile and trim, the main band, and the ears.

Color the top of the hat in alternate red and white stripes, leaving the button trim white. Make the ears pale green, then get some gray shading into the brim.

SHOULDER BAG

An everyday accessory could be this practical-looking shoulder bag, with a flap-over cover and buckle fastening, and a zip-fastened pocket on the front. Bags like this are very common, but an individual bag can come to be associated with a particular character. Note the way it hangs across from one shoulder to the opposite hip.

Add a double line for a shoulder strap over the shoulder and under the arm. Create a front and welt for the bag, adding trim details and buckles.

Draw a torso using basic shapes for joints and lines for bones, then flesh out the torso and arms. Outline a T-shirt and add a belt at the waist.

Ink the lines of the bag, outlining all the details of the belts and buckles, the pockets and name-badge holder. Ink some shading on the strap.

Leaving the buckles and trim white, and areas of white on the top of the bag to help with its overall shape, color the bag bright blue.

CRASH HELMET

Perhaps your character is a star race driver, or a space pilot. If so, they may need some smart headgear like this blue-and-yellow crash helmet. Helmets are usually a smooth, circular shape, and can have a cut-away face like this one, or be fully enclosed with just the eyes visible. The visor should fall down to the nose level, and may be tinted to reduce glare and reflection.

Start with an oval, then draw two lines down from it to a pointed chin. Add a neck, then create an eyeline. Refine the profile on the right, then draw in eyes with highlights, eyebrows, nose, and mouth.

Draw a large, circular shape to create the outline of a helmet. Add a horizontal across the forehead and bring this down on both sides to chin level, then round off. Finally, add the line of the base of the visor across the nose and out to both sides.

Use a medium nib to ink the outline of the helmet and visor. Then with a thinner pen, ink in stripe details and outline two stars. Finally, ink the eyes, eyebrows, and top of the nose.

Color the top of the helmet bright blue, with a pale blue side. Work the color around the stars. Color the stripe details gold. Make the eyes blue. Then shade the visor blue-gray.

ELBOW AND WRIST GUARDS

A teenage character might be speeding around on a skateboard, or inline skates, and if so he or she may need to wear protective accessories like these elbow guards and wrist supports. Notice how the elbow guard cups the elbow for maximum protection and comfort.

Refine the profile of a top, then work in a rounded protector over the elbow joint. Add the strap at the crook of the elbow. Next add a double band at the wrist.

Use circles for shoulder and elbow joints with lines for bones, then flesh out arms, with a thin wrist and hand with four fingers and a thumb. Flesh out a basic torso and the top of a leg.

Color the elbow pad purple, then use gray to get some shading into the white areas. Color the strap and the wrist-band brown, leaving a white highlight with gray shading.

Outline the elbow pad, then work the pattern on it. Add some stripes on the strap. Then ink the detail on the wrist guard.

KNEEPADS

These kneepads are an ideal accessory to go with the elbow guards. They are molded to fit the knee and protect against any crash landings your character may have to suffer. The striped grooves are designed to reduce the stress on the overall shape, as well as being a decorative touch. And they're fastened behind the knee with adjustable strapping.

Draw ovals for knee joints and lines for bones, then flesh out the profiles of two legs. Add boots to both legs.

Now create the knee pads, which are essentially triangles, with zigzag details. Indicate the strap at the back.

Ink the lines of the pads, taking care that they read as two separate pads, one for each knee with the front one slightly obscuring the back.

Working around the detailing at the top, color the main parts of the pads dark green, then use brown for the zigzag detail and the strap. Add some shading to the white details.

33

NERD GLASSES

Nerdy, intelligent characters are a familiar sight in manga stories, and these classic spectacles are an ideal way to suggest this type of personality. The shape of the lenses should be large and round, with simple thin wire frames that curl right around behind the ears. You can add a slight gradient tint and some white highlights to suggest reflection.

Create large round spectacles by drawing a couple of circles, then joining them with a bridge. Finally add an earpiece.

Draw a circle for the head, with lines down to a pointed chin. Add an eyeline and draw eyes and an ear to this line. Add a nose and mouth, and some spiky hair.

Outline the main lines of the spectacles in ink, then ink in the outlines of the iris.

Use a pale cool blue to get some color into the lenses, suggesting that they are made of glass.

CROSSED BELTS

A more swashbuckling look is this crossed-belt arrangement, slung down on either side of the hips. The belts can be contrasting colors. They have large buckles, and would be suitable for a cool, fashionable character or even a gunslinger. Note how the eyeholes are evenly spaced along the length of the belt.

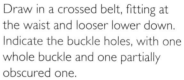

Create a basic torso from above the waist to above the knee. Draw a belt and fly. Then criss-cross the pants with lines to suggest creases.

Draw in a crossed belt, fitting at the waist and looser lower down. Indicate the buckle holes, with one whole buckle and one partially obscured one.

Define the outline of the belt, creating a three-dimensional profile at the top of both parts of the belt. Ink all the details.

Leaving the buckles white, color the belt using browns to indicate leather. Finally get some shading into the buckles using gray for a metallic look.

SCARF

In a blizzard, dust storm, or gas cloud, a face-covering scarf like this can be a useful accessory. It covers the nose and mouth, and folds around the neck where it's tied. Behind you can see the remainder of the scarf trailing in the breeze in two rippling strands, which gives a good dramatic visual effect.

Create a basic head, with a pointed chin and a suggestion of spiky hair. Add an eyeline and position eyes and ears. Square off the jaw and the top of the head.

Now start to cover the bottom of the nose, the mouth, and the neck area, and the top of the chest with a series of loose flowing lines of fabric.

Next add the two tails of the fabric, trailing out behind the figure to suggest movement.

Ink the lines of the fabric scarf, getting some movement into the folds and creases.

Finally, leaving white areas for highlights, use a bright red to color the scarf. Then use a darker red to get some shading into the folds in the fabric.

EYE PATCH

This eye patch and scar combination is a great way to give a character a menacing, thuggish aspect. The patch is held on by an elastic strap that runs diagonally across the head and behind the ear. The scar runs in a curve down from the nostril toward the lower jaw, and looks like it came from a fight. Note the shape of this character's head and features, which all add to the look. The shading on the eye patch is slightly graduated to give the impression of a curved surface.

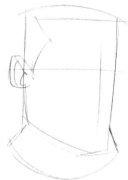

Use basic shapes to create a fairly square head with a pointed chin and simple hair profile. Add an eyeline and draw in an ear. Add a vertical center line.

Draw one eye and eyebrow on the eyeline. Add an eye patch where the second eye would be positioned, taking the strap out to the ear and up over the other eye. Add a nose and mouth.

To add to the character's air of mystery, draw in a black-and-blue scar with lines for the scars of stitches.

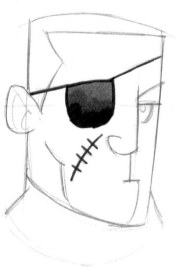

Ink the outline of the patch, the straps of the patch, and the lines of the scar.

Then color the eye patch very dark gray.

EARRING

Another type of jewelry you can dress your character with are earrings. These can be simple or more elaborate like these ornate examples. The stud is supporting a string of small beads, followed by a gem in a clasp, and some hook-shaped attachments in alternative colors.

Create the profile of an ear, paying attention to the whorls inside, and the basic shape of the lobe where the earring will sit.

Draw a circle on the earlobe, then a series of smaller circles for the jewels hanging down. Then add a large jewel.

To finish the drawing, add a few chunky U-shaped jewels.

Ink over all the lines of the earring, outlining the details.

Use ice blue to color some of the jewels, together with pale lime green. As you color, leave white highlights to suggest the shimmer on the jewels.

WRIST STRAPPINGS

Your manga character may be a street fighter, in which case he may wear these wrist wraps as a support accessory. They focus the viewer's attention on the hands, and emphasize the no-holds-barred attitude to combat that a street-fighter has, which can instill a nervous apprehension in an opponent and aid a fighter's victory.

Create a hand from basic shapes: circles for joints and lines for bones. Flesh out the hand. Add a long, thin wrist.

Add some pairs of lines from the knuckles to the top of the wrist. Keep the pairs randomly spaced but parallel to each other.

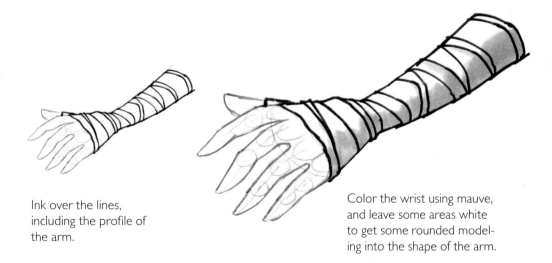

Ink over the lines, including the profile of the arm.

Color the wrist using mauve, and leave some areas white to get some rounded modeling into the shape of the arm.

GALLERY

hair ribbon

right A simple, pretty ribbon can add cuteness to any girl character, and add color and visual interest to her hair.

boot

above Sturdy, all-purpose boots are a must in all kinds of situations. They can be sturdy like this one, or more dainty for a cuter, more feminine look.

wings

below Fantasy is an important part of manga, so you could give your character a lift with a beautiful pair of wings.

bracelet

above Any girl can be given added glamour by adding some sparkling bangles and bracelets like these.

knife sheath

above This knife strapped onto the leg of an adventurous action girl could prove vital in a steamy jungle setting.

goggles

right Antiglare goggles like these could be useful in a polar landscape or a sun-drenched desert world.

headband

above Another interesting head accessory is this classic-looking headband. Use it for a royal princess or as part of a magical girl's armory.

necklace/amulet

above Jewelry adds a touch of glamour, and can also be a magical talisman for any girl.

vanity bag

above Feminine and functional, a bag like this could be used to carry vital ingredients for a magic spell. It needs to be carefully color-coordinated.

glove

left A thick, chunky glove is an ideal accessory for a fighter or a street character.

41

WEAPONS

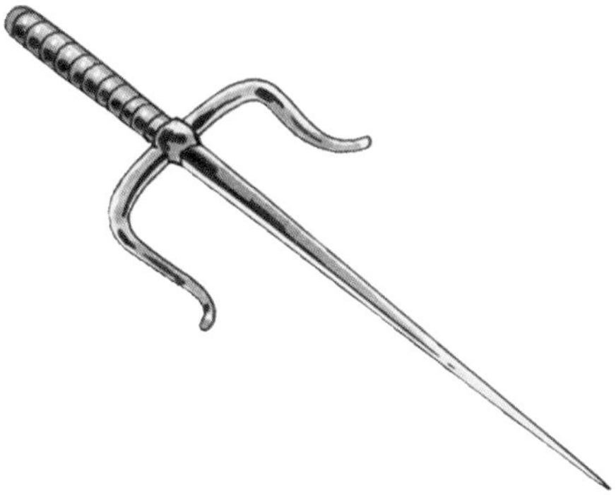

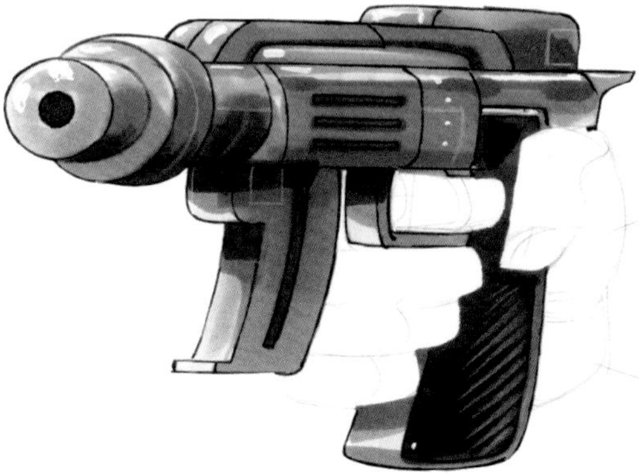

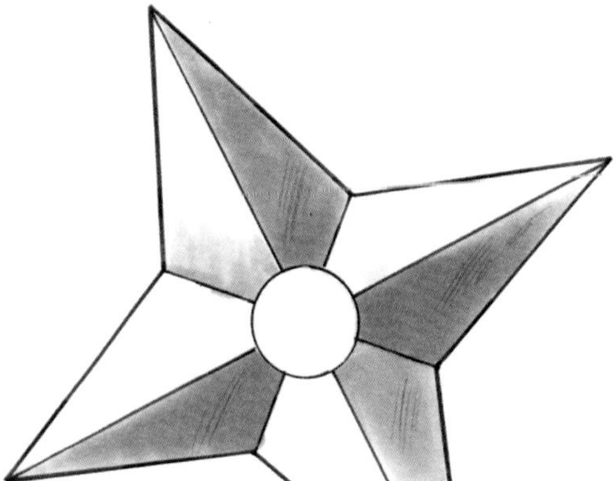

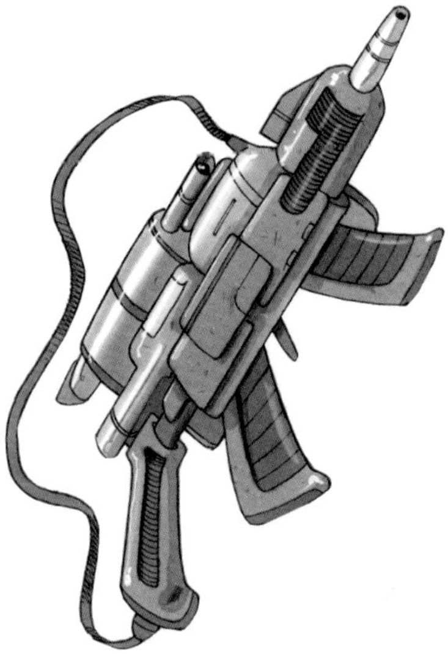

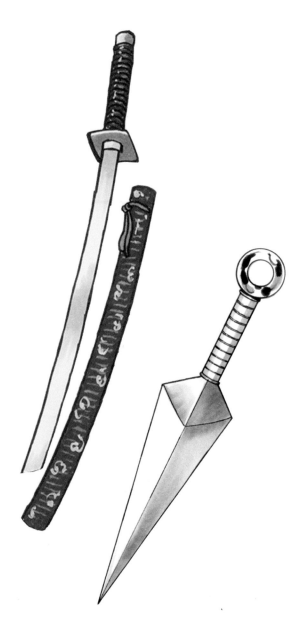

Weapons play a big part in action stories. As with other aspects of manga, many weapons are recognizable as real, but with elaboration or embellishments, while others are total fantasy or futuristic. Martial arts are common in manga stories, and weapons from these disciplines also appear often.

SHURIKEN THROWING STAR

Throwing stars like this are used by ninja warriors and martial arts fighters, and are sometimes known as *hira shuriken*. They are usually small enough to fit in the hand, and are held between the fingers in readiness for launching. Note how using shades of mauve-gray can give a good metallic sheen to your star.

  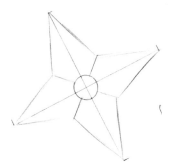

Start by drawing a circle, then cross it with two diagonal lines. Add a short line to the end of each, perpendicular to it.

Now add a short straight line from the circle out, in between the longer lines.

Then join the long and short lines to create a pointed star shape with the circle as its center.

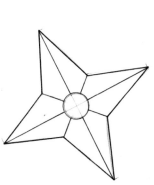

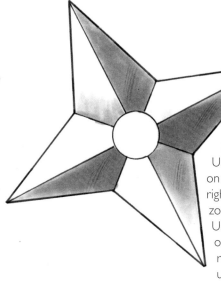

Ink the central circle, then all the main lines radiating from it. Also ink around the exterior.

Color the star using mauve-gray. Use stronger color on the faces on the right and the horizontal undersides. Use a paler purple on the top upper right horizontal and upper left vertical to create some modeling.

SHURIKEN THROWING DAGGER

These short daggers are also a throwing weapon, used in the same way as the star. They are small enough to sit between the fingers, and can be thrown in multiple volleys. *Shuriken* weapons are made in a variety of shapes. Note the grooved hilt, which helps the holder to keep a good grip, and the weighted end, which gives balance to the throw.

Draw one circle inside another, with a straight line to indicate the centerline of a blade.

Add in the outline of the hilt, crossing it with a series of horizontal lines. Thicken the line of the end of the hilt.

Now add in the diamond-shaped top of the blade.

Using a ruler, create the lines of the blade, coming to a sharp point at the end.

Ink over the main lines of the end, hilt, and the blade. Add some black shading on the circular end.

Use a steely mauve to color the blade, making one half darker than the other to indicate shading. Add some shading to the right-hand side of the hilt.

45

KATANA SWORD

This is another common weapon in manga stories featuring samurai warriors. The *katana* is a traditional Japanese sword, dating back to the 1400s, and is still used for ceremonial purposes today. It consists of a long, curving blade and hilt, and was often used in tandem with a shorter version for close fighting.

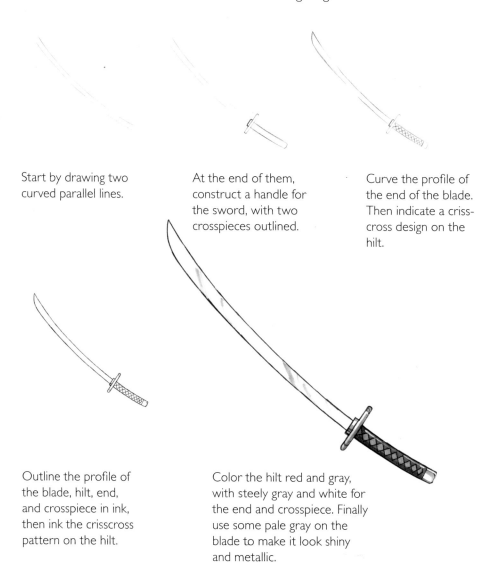

Start by drawing two curved parallel lines.

At the end of them, construct a handle for the sword, with two crosspieces outlined.

Curve the profile of the end of the blade. Then indicate a criss-cross design on the hilt.

Outline the profile of the blade, hilt, end, and crosspiece in ink, then ink the crisscross pattern on the hilt.

Color the hilt red and gray, with steely gray and white for the end and crosspiece. Finally use some pale gray on the blade to make it look shiny and metallic.

STAFF

A simple-looking staff like this can turn into a fearsome weapon in the hands of a master. Based on the traditional smaller three-section staff, or nunchaku, this heavyweight version can take out whole lines of opponents in a single sweep.

Draw a basic warrior figure in a martial stance. Give him two hands, and place a long stick created from parallel lines between them. Add a circular end.

Now create the detailing near the bottom end, and then repeat the shape at the top, and add similar detailing.

Ink the lines of the stick, the ends of the stick, and the details on the stick.

Add some initial shading onto the length of the stick, then gently shade the right-hand edges of the white tips to get some modeling here.

Working around the hands, color the stick black. Leave a highlight right down the center of the stick to help round it out. Finally, add gray highlights to the right of the white ends, again to help define their roundness.

FANTASY SWORD

In manga, you can let your imagination run wild, taking familiar objects and creating fantastic variants. This super-sized sword looks like it is completely unwieldy, but can be held by a single hand. The hilt is studded with jewels and is heavily decorated in gold. The blade itself is fearsome-looking, with a sharp cutaway section.

Start with a diagonal line, then bisect this with two lines perpendicular to it. Create a simple handle and a hand to clasp it, then indicate the top plate.

Refine the hilt details, outlining the top plate, and working up the handle details: the plate and end roundels.

Draw the curved blade, outlining it twice. Add details on the hilt end of the blade, here a triangle with circles, then add circle details to the broad plate.

Use gold for the main areas of the hilt and plate, then use red to pick out the details. Leave white highlights that could be jewels or metallic details. Finally, use an ice blue to create the metallic edges of the scimitar, and show where it is catching the light.

Ink all the important details around the hilt and on the blade, and ink around the plates. Outline the double edge of the blade and the cutout. Add shading in ink.

MAGIC SCEPTER

Another popular manga weapon is a magic-powered scepter. It is often used by female characters, and is a much less aggressive form of attack, utilizing bursts of light and flashes of crackling energy. The long handle can be highly ornamental and colorful, as seen in this example.

Begin by drawing an oval for the top of the weapon, then draw two verticals down to a point.

Starting at the top, add circular details. Define the line of the plate at the top. Add details halfway down, then add a couple of circular beads at the bottom.

Continue building up details on the stick. Then add some flowing ribbons hanging down from the top plate.

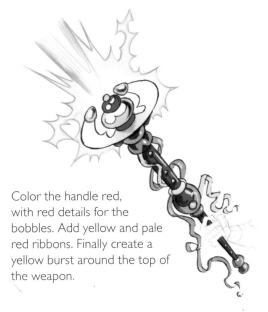

Use a fine pen to ink all the important lines, picking out details on all the various decorative elements. Outline the flowing ribbons.

Color the handle red, with red details for the bobbles. Add yellow and pale red ribbons. Finally create a yellow burst around the top of the weapon.

ARM PLASMA CANNON

Manga characters can be equipped with all kinds of electronic and technological weaponry. The basic rule is detailing—with mechanical hardware, the more the merrier! An arm-mounted cannon like this one, for instance, has a variety of shapes and features. It sits snugly around the forearm, with a high hand grip for stability and a low-slung nozzle for firing plasma bolts. The ammunition is fed through to the main weapon body from super-insulated tubing behind.

Create an arm from basic shapes for joints and lines for bones, then flesh it out and add a basic hand. Add a torso.

Now begin to sketch some rough shapes for a handle, and a rectangular block around the forearm, with further blocks underneath the arm.

Work in lots of details to give your drawing a mechanical look. Try and imagine the possible purpose of the pieces you add to make them more convincing. Add a suggestion of a nozzle, switches and controls, and a coiling tube behind the body.

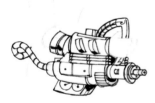

Next, ink your drawing, including some solid blacks to suggest shadows, and to give a metallic sheen to the cylindrical handle and arm support. Use a finer pen to ink the details such as the grooves on the tubing and on the handle.

Finally, color your drawing using shades of gray and mauve. Define the light source from above, with darker tones of gray on the underside of the weapon, and leave lighter highlights on the handle and tubing.

HAND BLASTER

A compact hand blaster is a good personal weapon in a manga tale of the future. This solid-looking example is composed of simple shapes, based on a contemporary handgun. The handle, or grip, should be shaped to fit comfortably in the hand, with a trigger positioned where it meets the barrel.

Start by drawing a gripping hand shape, with the index finger slightly separated, then sketch in the shape of the handle in a curving rectangle.

Draw a cylindrical barrel with two circles at its end, then work the other end of the barrel. Add detailing around the barrel.

Add the trigger and trigger guard, then build up the detail on the barrel and stock, and add a magazine chamber jutting down from the barrel in front of the trigger.

Ink all the main lines of your drawing and when the ink is dry, erase any pencil marks.

Color your weapon with dark grays for a solid, metallic look. Use a darker shade for the grip and detailing, and use some white highlights on top of the barrel to give added depth.

FINGER LASERS

For a more subtle and personal touch, your character could use these fingertip-mounted laser blasters. Each blaster sits snugly over the first joint of the finger, and is made from polished steel. Note the position of the hand for firing, and the soft blue light emanating from all the laser beams.

Draw a basic hand shape from lines and circles for joints, then define the joints as more rectangular. Make the thumb read as separate.

Add circles to the ends of the fingers and thumb. Then define the joints more closely and sharpen the profile of the palm.

Now lightly indicate the laser beams coming from the nozzles on each fingertip.

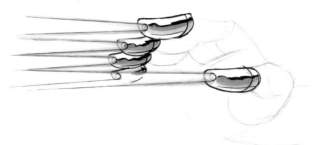

Ink the joints of the thumb, then ink the other finger joints.

Create rounded profiles using white, black, and gray, with touches of blue. Then color the lasers using pale blue.

ASSAULT RIFLE

A sturdier field weapon could be this solid assault rifle, with shoulder strap and telescopic sight. The rifle has a grip, a stock, and a magazine chamber at the front, and the overall shape is bulky and heavy, to emphasize the idea of a powerful piece of hardware.

Start with three basic shapes, for the barrel, grip, and magazine.

Add a cylinder shape to the end of the barrel, with a thinner muzzle and sight, then draw a stock on the rear, pointing diagonally down.

Build up the detail on the barrel, adding a telescopic sight and a trigger, with molding on the grip and magazine.

Finish the drawing with a snaking shoulder strap.

Ink the drawing, including all the fine details.

Lastly, color the rifle with purples and grays, adding white highlights to the top areas, then use darker gray to color the molding below.

GALLERY

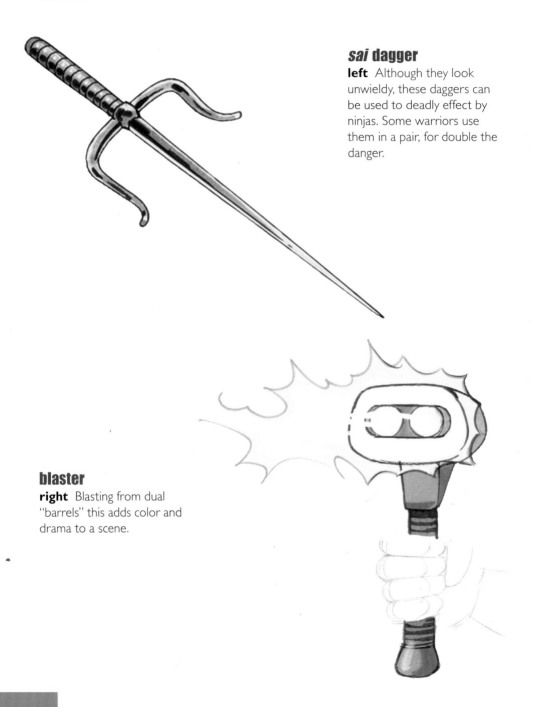

sai dagger

left Although they look unwieldy, these daggers can be used to deadly effect by ninjas. Some warriors use them in a pair, for double the danger.

blaster

right Blasting from dual "barrels" this adds color and drama to a scene.

buzz bomb

left With wings and antennae, this weapon could be launched at an enemy by remote and guided in.

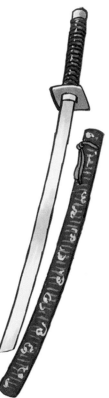

katana sword

right *Katana* swords date back to feudal times in Japan. They are a standard weapon in many action manga stories.

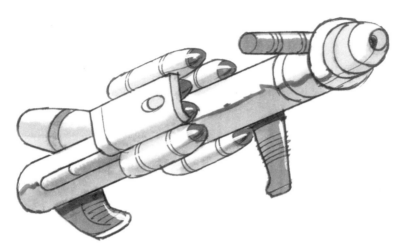

rapid fire

above With features reminiscent of a spaceship, this
futuristic weapon would work
for any space warrior.

handgun

right This model is based
on a standard handgun with
stock, trigger, and barrel. It is
suitable for many storylines.

multibarrel

left This is a serious-looking weapon, packing a ton of fire power. The character's intentions are clear.

ray gun

below A stunner or phaser is based on a regular hand-gun, which can be any color. This one is more suitable for a space-age story line.

VEHICLES

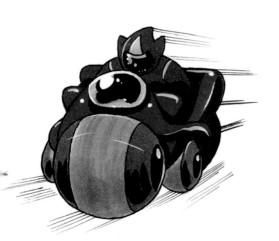

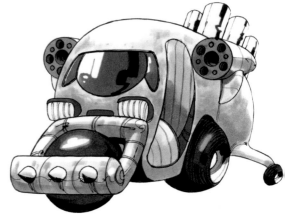

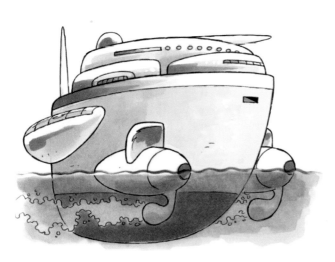

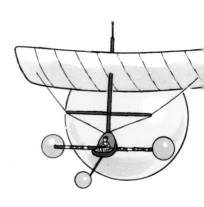

You can really let your imagination go wild when it comes to vehicles. You can start with something that is real, such as a car or plane, and then customize it as you see fit. If your stories feature space travel and futuristic scenes, there is no limit to what you can draw. Practice these examples to get yourself going.

MOBILE PATROL BATTLE ARMOR

Fighting armor and battle suits feature in many sci-fi manga stories. Here is an idea for a patrol vehicle, equipped with sensors, cameras, and cannon lasers. The jointed legs can extend to full height to give extra width of vision. The hands comprise three fast-rotating impact blasters for a scatter-gun attack. The pilot sits in the egg-shaped capsule at the top, with twin visibility apertures.

Start by drawing two torpedo shapes, one on top of the other.

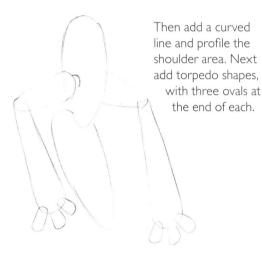

Then add a curved line and profile the shoulder area. Next add torpedo shapes, with three ovals at the end of each.

From the left-hand oval, create an upcurving joint and a downward point of attachment for two round wheels.

Add details to the pilot capsule, with twin apertures, and a shoulder-mounted cannon. Draw a telescopic motion sensor stalk on the central unit, and add some fine line detailing on the limbs.

Finish your pencil drawing with some stabilizing fins on the back, and connect your shoulder-cannon with a curling lead.

Lastly, color your battle armor, using a soft beige to give shadow and depth to the white body parts, and a darker clay color for contrasting stripes. The apertures should be colored with a blue-gray, and the wheels should be dark gray.

Ink your drawing carefully, adding some solid black to the apertures at the top for a reflective Perspex look.

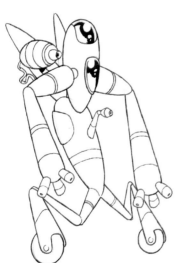

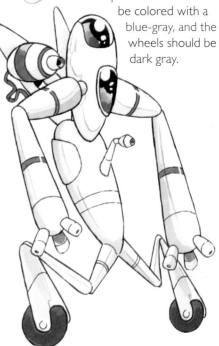

HIGH-SPEED APPREHENSION UNIT

This is a fast, agile unit for high-speed pursuit. Its low, wide shape gives extra stability in a chase, and its flat, squat wheels are excellent for all terrain. The front of the vehicle is equipped with high-velocity static-shock cannons, which can disable the electronic systems of a fleeing vehicle at a distance of 3 miles (4.8 km). The shielding canopy is designed to withstand aerial bombardment and doubles up as a solar panel for extra fuel efficiency.

Start by drawing a rectangle, then create a curved front.

Next outline a wheel at each corner, using basic shapes. Make the wheels at the front smaller than those at the back.

Add detail for the passenger well and roof. Then on the near underside create engineering details. Add a shield canopy to the top.

Finish your drawing by adding two static-shock cannons on the front of the unit.

Ink the lines of your car. The inking can be very simple, except for the engine detailing under the car.

Color the wheels in shades of dark gray to show their roundness. Make the body of the car red, with a white stripe and a white shield on top. Keep the cannons white, and use a shade of beige to suggest shape.

RIOT BUSTER

This is a vehicle designed for breaking up public disturbances in confined urban streets. It is compact and built for single-operator use. The spiked battering ram at the front will quickly clear a path through an unruly mob, and the twin rocket launchers on either side of the cab can unleash multiple volleys of resin pellets, which are nonfatal but very effective. The rear "exhaust" pipes are for spraying tear gas over a wide area.

Start with a large oval, and a small circle cutting at the bottom left.

Draw the battering ram around the front circle, and add a curving rectangle for a door.

Add a full, rippling skirt Behind the door, add a large wheel, and a smaller stabilizing wheel at the rear. Draw two rocket launchers, one on either side of the unit down to just above ankle level.

Next, add spikes to the battering ram, and four exhaust pipes protruding from the rear. Draw in some headlights, and indicate the curve of a seat in the cabin.

Ink all the main lines of your drawing, and give a chrome look to the exhaust by using a wavy solid black line. A brush pen is good for this.

Color using a dull mauve-gray for the body, with a darker gray for the wheels and a cream for the internal upholstery. Add a little yellow to the headlights.

TROOP-DISPERSAL CARRIER

This is an aerial troop-carrier that can transport huge armies across long distances. The curving teardrop shape gives the impression of a menacing insect in flight, creating a sense of unease in any opposing forces. The carrier is driven by two giant propeller engines, and underneath is the dispersal pod for unloading. On the top of the fuselage is a control and observation deck.

Start with a large semielliptical shape, with a shallow semi-circle underneath.

Add two ellipses to the top of the vehicle. These lines define the vehicle as a plane and form its cabin, wings, and fuselage.

Work up some detail, adding in the cockpit and two propellers.

Indicate windows in the cabin, and rede-fine the nose cone. Add the light to the upper carriage.

Ink all the main lines, to show the detailing in the cabin and fuselage where sheets have been joined. Outline the windows, then use black to create the whirring motion of the propellers.

Color the vehicle using sand. Color the nose cone, the center of the propellers, and the tail fin gold, with red for the light.

EXPLORATORY CONVOY TRAIN

This is a vehicle widely used during mankind's expansion into outer space. It can cope with all kinds of hostile atmospheres, and its super-thick shell is designed to cope with a wide range of gravitational pressures. The train can carry all the necessary building tools and supplies needed to sustain a human colony for several years, and can carry up to a thousand individuals. The giant caterpillar tracks are flexible enough to cope with unpredictable terrain.

Start with a two-point perspective block, with a line going off onto the horizon.

Use these perspective lines to help you create a series of carriages. They grow smaller as they recede into the distance.

On the front of the train, draw a large caterpillar tread and add some rectangular blocks on either side of the carriages.

Next, draw the blasters on the far side of the lead carriage. Add some grooves for windows, some wheels, and indicate an elevator boarding tube on the right, with some small figures to show scale.

Ink your drawing carefully, using some small lines to indicate texture on the train and also on the ground.

Finally, color with dull gray-beige, and charcoal gray for the caterpillar tracks. Use a little sand color for the ground, and add some cool gray shadows around the blasters.

MOBILE ENVIRONMENT

Other worlds may be unable to sustain human life. This mobile, self-contained habitat can be used to explore while enabling the population to live a reasonably normal existence. The main dome contains a large-sized natural environment, with fields, trees, mountains, and rivers, and can accommodate a city-sized population. The smaller, secondary dome contains a miniature sea. The whole environment travels on a series of omnidirectional spherical wheels.

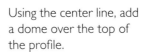

Draw a vertical center line, then create a low oval out to each side.

Using the center line, add a dome over the top of the profile.

Draw in a central apron to ground level, then on either side add a series of wheels. Add some trunking on the apron.

Sketch in some mountains, trees, and hills in the main dome, and an indication of water in the small one.

Ink your drawing, indicating some reflective spots on the dome, and some solid blacks between the wheels.

Color your drawing, using gray for the vehicle base, and blues, mauves, and greens for the natural environment.

CRUISE SHIP

This craft is built to take large numbers of people on pleasure cruises around the polluted oceans of a future earth. The seawater is toxic, so the ship has to be completely enclosed and sit high up out of the water to avoid contamination of any passengers. It is driven by two side-mounted jet engines, which churn through the stagnant waters. On the left toward the rear is the viewing cabin, which is the nearest the passengers can safely get to the sea.

Create a curved irregular polygon, and lightly indicate a water line.

Add details of a cabin on the deck, together with some portholes for passengers to gather behind.

Now add two large jet-propulsion engines on either side, and indicate the churning water in their wake.

Draw a viewing cabin at the rear, and add portholes and a forward antenna at the top.

Ink your drawing, including all the portholes and the wake behind the propulsion units.

Color the main body of the ship yellow, with white upper cabins and viewing cabin. Use gray for some shading, and color the sea with a dirty-looking gray blue, light enough so that you can still see the bottom of the ship.

GALLERY

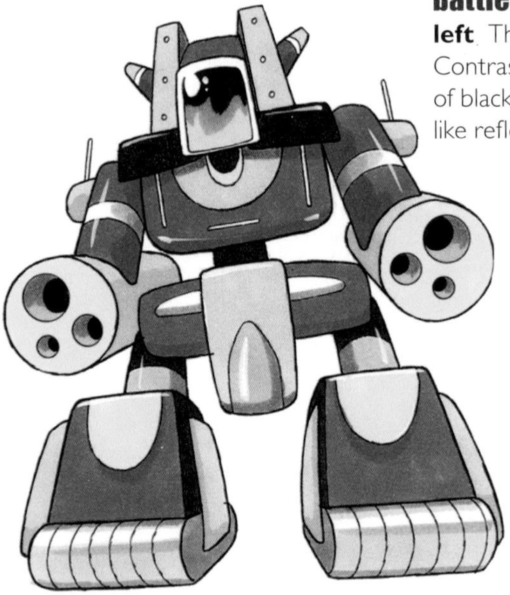

battle suit

left This vehicle is based on a humanoid shape. Contrasting colors give it impact, while a touch of black on the main surfaces makes them look like reflective plastic.

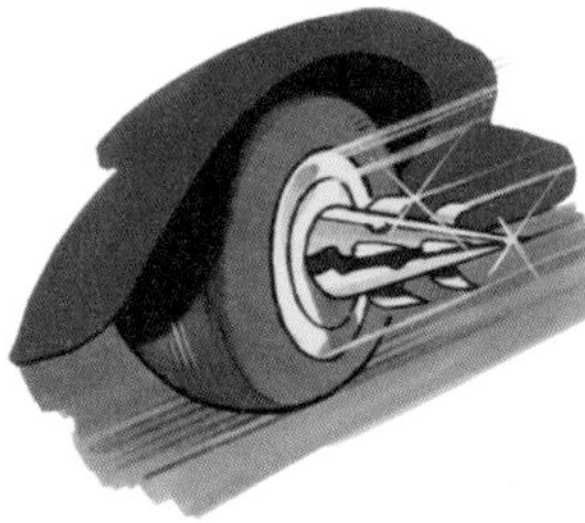

spiked bike

above Part-weapon, part-vehicle, this craft has spikes that could destroy a pursuing vehicle without any trouble: it shreds tires, tracks, and anything else that gets in the way.

space saucer

right A vehicle like this one can fly, possibly even in space. It looks slightly menacing, with its dangling tentacles, curved wings, and green color.

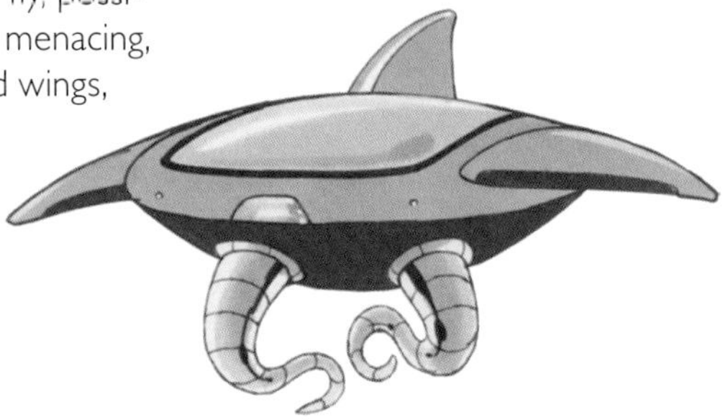

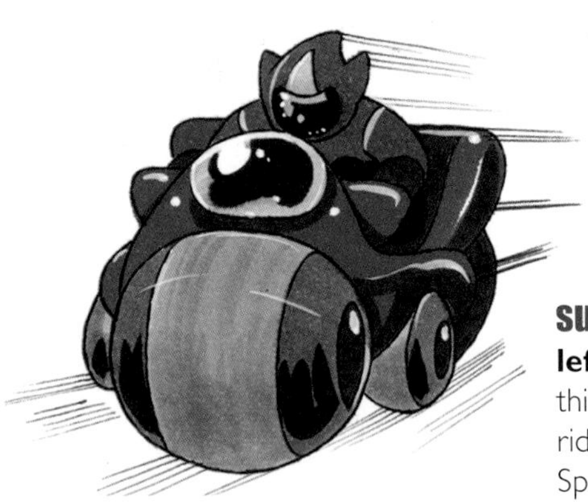

superbike

left There is no sign of any weapons on this three-wheeled bike with a dark, sinister rider—but there's no hitching a ride either. Speed lines give the bike some motion.

flying cruiser

right A huge, futuristic transport plane, this has a vast hold for goods, as well as a large passenger cabin. The shiny metallic finish suggests it is capable of reaching high speeds.

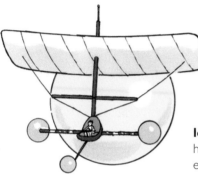

left A single-seat flying machine powered by helium, this could belong in a story set in a futuristic ecological society.

military style

right Dull colors work well for noncivilian vehicles. This slow-moving armored military craft can hold and move several personnel over long distances.

hover boat

left A fun-looking one-man hoverboat dashes across the water. Here the splashing water, together with speed lines and the hair streaming behind the driver, combine to give a sense of speed.

GLOSSARY

accessory A thing that can be added to something else to make it more useful or attractive.

agile Able to move quickly and easily.

amulet An ornament or small piece of jewelry thought to give protection against evil, danger, or disease.

aperture An opening, hole, or gap; a space through which light passes in an optical or photographic instrument.

armory Arsenal.

austere A severe or strict manner, attitude, or appearance; having an extremely plain and simple style or appearance.

bangle A rigid bracelet or anklet.

bewildering Causing someone to become perplexed and confused.

bleed To seep into an adjacent color or area.

bobble A small ball made of strands of wool used as a decoration on a hat or furnishings.

chevron A line or stripe in the shape of a V or an inverted V.

denote To indicate or be a sign of.

ellipse A two-dimensional shape like a stretched circle with slightly longer flatter sides.

emanate To come from or come out of somebody, something, or somewhere; to emit or send out, such as rays.

feral Gone wild; for example, animals or plants that live or grow in the wild after having been domestically reared.

freehand Done by hand and without using drawing instruments such as rulers or compasses.

fuselage The body of an airplane, containing the cockpit, passenger seating, and cargo hold but not including the wings.

gauntlet A glove with a long wide cuff that covers and protects part of the forearm.

gouache A type of painting that uses opaque pigments ground in water and thickened with a gluelike substance.

gradient A fade from one color to another.

hira shuriken Throwing stars; flat, wheel-shaped plates of metal with sharpened points or edges.

infrared The portion of the invisible electromagnetic spectrum consisting of radiation, between light and radio waves.

katana nunchaku A long, curved single-edged sword traditionally used by Japanese samurai.

menace A possible source of danger.

nib A sharp point or tip of a pen, by means of which the ink is transferred to the paper.

nonconformist An unconventional person; one who does not conform to an accepted pattern of behavior.

paper weight In expressing paper density, paper weight is expressed in grams per square meter (g/m^2), which is used in many countries. In the United States, it is expressed in terms of mass per number of sheets, called basis weight. The conversion is pounds of a ream of 500 sheets of a given basis size. Japanese paper is usually expressed as the weight in kilograms of 1,000 sheets.

perspective The theory or practice of allowing for the appearance of objects to an observer, allowing for the effect of their distance from the observer, when drawing or painting.

plasma A hot ionized gas made up of ions and electrons that is found in the sun, stars, and fusion reactors.

profile The outline of somebody's face as seen from the side.

protrude To stick out from the surroundings, or make something do this.

resin A substance that is secreted in the sap of some plants and trees and that is used in varnishes, paints, and inks; a compound that looks like natural resin and that is used to manufacture plastics.

***sai* dagger** A pointed, dagger-shaped metal martial arts weapon.

samurai An aristocratic Japanese warrior of a class that dominated the military aristocracy between the eleventh and nineteenth centuries.

scimitar A saber or sword.

surveillance Continual observation of a person or group.

swashbuckler A bold and swaggering swordsman or adventurer.

talisman An object believed to give magical powers to someone who carries or wears it, such as a stone or jewel.

thong A thin strip of leather used for fastening or supporting things.

tone A shade of color.

whorl One turn in a spiral.

FOR MORE INFORMATION

Cartoon Art Museum
655 Mission Street
San Francisco, CA 94105
(415) CAR-TOON [227-8666]
Web site: http://cartoonart.org
The Cartoon Art Museum has more than 6,000 pieces of
    original cartoon and animation art in its collection. It also has
    a comprehensive research library, and exhibition galleries.

Japanese Canadian Cultural Centre (JCCC)
6 Garamond Court
Toronto, ON M3C 1Z5
Canada
(416) 441-2345
Web site: http://www.jccc.on.ca
The JCCC provides opportunities to the public for meeting
    and for exchanging ideas about Japanese art and cultural
    programs in the Japanese-Canadian community.

Japan Foundation, Los Angeles
333 South Grand Avenue, Suite 2250
Los Angeles, CA 90071
(213) 621-2267

Web site: http://www.jpf.go.jp/jfla
This institution provides a variety of programs that relate to
    Japanese studies, language, arts, and media.

Japan Society, New York
333 East 47th Street
New York, NY 10017
(212) 832-1155
Web site: http://www.japansociety.org
This nonprofit organization works to bring the people of
    Japan and the United States closer together through
    numerous activities and exchange programs, including film
    programs, art galleries, language programs, and lectures.

Kyoto International Manga Museum
Karasuma-Oike
Nakagyo-ku
Kyoto 604-0846
Japan
+81-75-254-7414
Web site: http://www.kyotomm.jp/english
The museum collects, researches, and studies manga-
    related materials, and promotes learning about the
    history of manga.

Museum of Comic and Cartoon Art (MoCCA)
594 Broadway, Suite 401
New York, NY 10012
(212) 254-3511
Web site: http://www.moccany.org

MoCCA collects, preserves, studies, and displays comic and cartoon art and illustration.

TOKYOPOP
5900 Wilshire Boulevard, Suite 2000
Los Angeles, CA 90036-5020
(323) 692-6700
Web site: http://www.tokyopop.com
TOKYOPOP was founded in 1997 by Stu Levy, and established a market for manga in North America. The company has published more than 3,000 books. It has produced live-action and animated film and television content based on its intellectual property library.

VIZ Media, LLC
295 Bay Street
San Francisco, CA 94133
Web site: http://www.viz.com
VIZ is an American entertainment company specializing in manga and anime. It has published some of the most well-known and popular manga magazines and titles.

WEB SITES

Due to the changing nature of Internet links, Rosen Publishing has developed an online list of Web sites related to the subject of this book. This site is updated regularly. Please use this link to access the list:

www.rosenlinks.com/mm/wva

FOR FURTHER READING

Brenner, Robin E. *Understanding Manga and Anime.* Westport, CT: Libraries Unlimited, 2007.

Cook, Trevor, and Lisa Miles. *Drawing Manga* (Drawing Is Fun!). New York, NY: Gareth Stevens Publishing, 2011.

Giannotta, Andrés Bernardo. *How to Draw Manga.* Mineola, NY: Dover, 2010.

Hart, Christopher. *Magical Girls and Friends: How to Draw the Super-Popular Action-Fantasy Characters of Manga.* New York, NY: Watson-Guptill, 2006.

Hart, Christopher. *Manga for the Beginner: Everything You Need to Start Drawing Right Away!* New York, NY: Watson-Guptill, 2008.

Hart, Christopher. *Mecha Mania: How to Draw Warrior Robots, Cool Spaceships, and Military Vehicles.* New York, NY: Watson-Guptill, 2002.

Hart, Christopher. *Young Artists Draw Manga.* New York, NY: Watson-Guptill, 2011.

Koyama-Richard, Brigitte. *One Thousand Years of Manga.* New York, NY: Rizzoli, 2008.

Lenburg, Jeff. *The Encyclopedia of Animated Cartoons.* 3rd ed. New York, NY: Facts On File, 2008.

Marcovitz, Hal. *Anime* (Eye on Art). Detroit, MI: Lucent Books, 2008.

McCarthy, Helen. *The Art of Osamu Tezuka*. DVD ed. New York, NY: Abrams ComicArts, 2009.

Nagatomo, Haruno. *Draw Your Own Manga: Beyond the Basics*. Tokyo, Japan: Kodansha International, 2005.

Okabayashi, Kensuke. *Manga for Dummies*. Hoboken, NJ: Wiley Publishing, 2007.

Okuma, Hidefumi. *Let's Draw Manga: Ninja and Samurai*. Kindle ed. Gardena, CA: Digital Manga Publishing, 2009.

Richmond, Simon. *The Rough Guide to Anime 1* (Rough Guide Reference). New York, NY: Rough Guides, 2009.

Samurai and Ninja Action Scene Collection. Tokyo, Japan: Graphic-Sha Publishing, 2007.

Sautter, Aaron, and Cynthia Martin. *How to Draw Manga Warriors* (Edge Books). Mankato, MN: Capstone Press, 2008.

Thompson, Jason. *Manga: The Complete Guide*. New York, NY: Del Rey, 2007.

INDEX

ABOUT THE AUTHORS

Anna Southgate is an experienced writer and editor who has worked extensively for publishers of adult illustrated reference books. Her recent work has included art instruction books and providing the text for a series of six manga titles.

Keith Sparrow has read and collected comics since he was a child. He has created hundreds of storyboards, including one for the animation movie *Space Jam*, and illustrated several children's educational books for the UK's Channel 4 and the BBC. He became a fan of manga and anime after reading *Akira*.

31901050814799